Table of Contents:

Preface:	Page 2
Face:	Page 9
Postface:	Page 74

Copyright 2013
All rights reserved.

Dedicated to Rumi who had kings as benefactors and all the others who got it and didn't have to shill to sell it.

AF472221

Preface:

Nothing like staring an expectation based on past practice and protocol in the face to tell you loud and clear that its value is questionable at best. So I stand on the precipice of this preface wondering how all these prefixes of 'pre' can creep into something that has clearly passed 'pre', the point of prior to emerging and is now buzzing around our ears like an untended and not otherwise predisposed fly.

Ah yes, the point. Well, back on point: which typically of a preface is to provoke as many book sales as possible I suppose, maybe to humor an author with the reputational size that garners spoiling, but in this case isn't either: the preface to Los Dichos (or whatever I end up calling it) is an attempt to explain that the words and concepts we use to explain how consciousness emerges into being and our experiential feel for this are in fact the enemy to the to the process (see? It's not a process! unless process can be conceived as an instantaneous quantum moment of reemergence sigh). Process is a great word, but it limits quantum possibilities to imagination and dreams, an incorrect assumption that leads to a kind of quantum blindness, an inability to see a world where emergence doesn't always get foreshadowed.

I guess the only remaining question is how many words I will throw, like good money after bad, trying to make that point as clearly as I can: words, even (or 'specially) those that attempt to explain being human serve a different master. The words shine light in false corners. They divert and muddy the clear waters of being. They serve ego which would have you believe that this (and you) are somehow it. Our best chance for triangulating being, words, end up being Igor and the resultant 'life' created on less optimistic days isn't kindly thought of as Frankenstein's monster, but as the dark abomination that it is. Words, sent to the laboratory by mind to select the proper mind for being human, gracelessly, complicitly, and without so much as a "my bad" to either the good doctor or the life that emerged, played fate's hand as dealt.

The alternatives don't play out well over distance, but might be considered for P2P moments like when the grid crashes and all the 'lectronics die. Here's one: look in another person's eyes, without talking and without anything else (either interpersonal or say background music or insence). That'll do ya. Another quieter, more subtle way is just sharing proximity, no talking, moving, just sharing proximity. Mebbe there's some psychic stuff also, right? Dream work. Remote viewing. But honestly, if you get to those levels then you're right back into the word game because you're going to have to carve off a generous slice of ego before the tricks of consciousness, once realized, lose their self-aggrandizing charms. Indeed the same paradoxical game that words play (necessary for communication yet utterly hopeless as a mechanism themselves) will play out with any of the psychic superpowers. But it takes words to mention this. The same words that poison the well of being. Igor words.

So jumping back in to the preface to ground the book: one way to be human is to imagine that this world, the world of senses and thoughts, the world of reality is a poisonous illusion. How could it be poisonous? I can see where chemical stuff and pollution is poisonous. I can see where things like war and social injustice might be considered poisonous, but you seem to be painting with a very broad brush and I can think of all sorta' things like hummingbirds and sunsets and the smell of the desert after rain, even the smell of the rain itself when it is thinking about hurdling the dry humidity and trying to quench the earth without drying on the way down from heaven. I mean if we were all first time cannabis buzzing, I'd probably totally get you, but that ship has sailed, so I need a rationale (told you 'bout the poison of words. Howse 'rationale' for ya?)

The world's poisonous nature is derived from you, kiddo. Sorry 'bout that. Without you, the world just kinda sits there, certainly in motion, changing, remember billions of years have passed (as near as we can figger) on this planet and the universe (as near as we can figger) preceded this planet by billions of years, however, that being said, we figure Indians came across a Siberian land bridge in 1...err 3...waves 15,000 years ago and those 43 or so people then spread from head to foot of the Americas, developed all the languages and families of Amerindians and a population of 50-100 million people by the time the greedy people with their bad germs arrived. A convenient history, since it wasn't civilized and they'd only been here a little while themselves, dominant culture genocide wasn't THAT bad, right? Anyway, the Canadians did it too and they're nice people. Point: history is written by the conquerors and when this perspectivized inaccurate version isn't available, it tends to be even sketchier.

So the world is just indifferently being and then YOU drop in. Now, some stuff is noticeable (worth noticing) and other stuff is not (hence of less importance). The noticeable stuff is rarely indifferent to YOU, otherwise you wouldn't notice it. Instead it falls into two basic categories, good and bad. 15,000 years ago when the first indigenous person (homeless at that) illegally crossed into the country (we have it on video I'm sure) good or bad had already crept like a stealthy mold off of the simple survival of the self (although some reasonable doubt exists as to whether 'the self' at that juncture was a person, family, or tribe). SO beyond good = life and bad = death, we had an emerging artistic value good/bad, an aesthetic sensory good/bad, and others. All, we are assured by our sociologists and evolutionists (and ultimate Freud and probably the Tea Party too) can be nicely tied back to life/death.

And at some digressive point we get love/hate emerging from life/death and then commerce gets involved and we have taken an inherently neutral kaleidoscopic panorama of universe and used our discriminative powers to tag the universe 'like' as well as 'dislike'. Of course very few things or people are universally liked or disliked and so we push and tug against competing opinions and go to life-fixated lengths to surround ourselves with that which our trainers/parents/media/overlords saw fit to designate as fashionable.

And right in the middle of this nest of ego, this web of ego, this cat's cradle of ego, this shadow game of ego lie words. Not lay words because what do words do in this web of deceit? They lie. They tell us cute is awesome.

Corvettes are stylish. Enlightenment is a noble pursuit. Guns are freedom. Terrorists are freedom fighters are terrorists (aren't they all just killers?!?) and other assorted tripe. When they get blown up to cartoon proportions, say Miley Cyrus heights, perhaps it seems more obvious that we're getting played, however that same player games every word and every idea from its runaway perspective of life/death that has spun into the bowerbird decorated brutally inescapable web we've imagined with our minds and built by words.

So throwing good money after bad, writing books of words knowing that words are the key ingredients of the poison of the illusion of ego that turns something as okay as being alive and being aware of it into that thing that we've each turned it into, a Frankensteinian monster of artificially conflated meanings based on a narrow-minded, data-poor interpretation of our experience.

A quick aside before I turn you loose, one of the cool things about self-publishing is that I get to choose the font size, resulting in a book I can read without magnification. At every turn, this book reflects that cooking without an editor mentality, and so your experience, if you choose to go farther will reflect the frustrations of my bias that over-tinkering is a synonym for professional perfectionism and my preference to tumbling rocks and transcribing the muses'

musings to finetooth combing material into something a froghair more palatable for anyone who might dive under the covers with a flashlight and see what the muses have told me. Click save and print, 11/11/13.

Los Dichos:

Your core beliefs are your largest bets. For people who pride themselves on conservatism, maturity, and logic, the degree of probability of these foundational beliefs paying off is akin to holding the only winning ticket in the mega lottery. A lot of you believe, deep down inside, that if you can control the universe you will be perfectly safe and validated as a worthy human being. Hence reincarnation. Here's another pile of chips, don't bet the house on 13 red. It doesn't even exist...

A universe of an infinite number of parallel perspectives suggests that an infinite number of parallel universes might be an unnecessary redundancy, however the tendency for fractal replication as well as our doubtlessly limited perspective argue otherwise, so maybe both.

Existential Limitation: Nothing we perceive exists solely within the range of our ability to perceive/experience it: light, sound, temperature, the vastness of our planet, space, the smallness of our cells, atoms. Why should our identity fall within the bounds of our

perception? Search below the chemical building blocks. Search high above the quantum magic.

Might the relative subjectivity of the individual human experience be serving a universal need rather than individual karma? Maybe the variety of perspectives is the universal consciousness version of 3-D glasses. Or maybe the universe has its own karma to attend to. It isn't always about us. A human-centric universe is egocentric sketchiness at its finest.

That we're living in a universe that so completely delivers the reality we each expect to see to each of us in all our diversity is truly marvelous. That we seem unaware, from an observatory standpoint as well as from a manifestive standpoint that we each receive a unique version is a bit perplexing. Perhaps the reality it provides is so complete that we fail to recognize the customization we experience?

Compassion may be conceived of as the awareness that all humans, all conscious life, whether it is karmic or nature/nurture or Truman Show paranoid nightmare is moment

by moment acting out an elaborate and complex caricature of who they think they are supposed to be. Inspiration for their role is drawn from a variety of demographic, cultural, biological, and conscious and unconscious prompting and from this infinite ongoing calculus, we act what we believe is our identity. Compassion is realizing this is not who we are; that the supposed identity is false, and loving each as their own expression of who they believe themselves to be, knowing that their true identity is the single-pointed vastness of the all.

For all self realization can be considered to be pulling the sword from the stone. Harmonizing in grace with all being may be conceived as the search for the grail. In recognizing the nature of the kingdom, we may sense that our proclamations have always alchemized from the throne and this may steady our rule and our hand.

If perspective is not accounted for in reality, then the stoplight is red for everyone and unnecessary delays in being ensue.

That you are surrounded by a world that will always exceed your ability to comprehend

and fully appreciate might fill you with ever-present wonder. That you get the chance might fill you with tears of gratitude.

...we loved the sun so much for its warmth and safety and missed it so much at night, we took little brother fire home to bed with us. that was the night we split from nature and began to tune out the fundamental messages of the universe, starting with the songs of the stars.

Uncrushed by the collective need for happier endings, simply being is cause for exuberance.

Being born into sentient being, in this universe of matter, is rarer than the least probable of lotteries. How do we begin to pay it back? What can we offer the universe in exchange for the gift of being? Sharing food, compassion, and shelter seems a wise start. A living wage might apply to the top end of the scale also. Anything more is not necessary. Quality of life is simply being and its awareness.

Given all the tones and hues, textures and spaces of the universe and of you, all that has been recognized and all that remains to be discovered, all the utility and all that is pre-conceptual utility, what then may you and the universe manifest? What magic may you both create? How much love might emerge in the space and time where you exist?

I'm not sure who created the universe or that it matters. I am sure who creates meaning. You create yours. And that it matters because your created meaning impacts the whole tribe.

The basics:
You alone can make your life magic.
You alone can make it not so."

Each moment in life's relationship bears the potential to emphatically conclude: "This is what I am here for." And every moment.

A glimmer of the wonder of the universe, that special someone perhaps, or a tremendous victory, begs us to consider the whole as such; a

spark to ignite a fire of wonder and passion as we give ourselves to the field which envelopes us, the field to which that which inspires our total passion is but a glimpse.

Years of fishing taught me that not all catches are keepers. My best application for this is my thoughts. I pretty much have to throw them all back, not because they're too small, or out of season, but because they come from polluted waters.

If you want to understand in order to control, good luck with that; if you want to understand in order to love, you will not have to rely upon luck.

Consciousness when freed of egoic delusion, clutter and burden is amazingly buoyant and ethereal.

Love in its simplest sense is a surrender of the self to the flow of being.

Happiness, dependent upon subjectively determined criteria, is constantly available for

your pleasure. Yet I count the letting go of happiness as a liberation point in this life. When happiness gets no more or less appreciation than any other state of being, for some reason it tends to stop teasing you and hang out for a while.

Maybe it's not the uniqueness of one's identity that is the basis of esteem, but instead the appreciation that in each moment the universe is unfolding uniquely for your perspective. Nobody gets to see through those eyes but you. Nobody.

We live in a world of undefined. We can spend our lives trying to define it. We can simply marvel in being. We live in a world of undefined. Whattya reckon we ought to do next? Let's define it indefinable and snuggle a while. That star just winked at me 5 billion years ago; it knew I was going to be watching.

Thinking is to sentience what dialing is to a phone call. A correctly dialed phone call where meaningful information is accurately shared: that's sentience.

The basic problem with reductionistic thinking is that the font gets so small, no one can understand the meaning.

The dispossession of false ownership is ultimate freedom. Willing or not, that which is not yours will be wrest from you, tangible or supposed: grateful appreciation to a universe willing to dedicate the personal time necessary for such unraveling of nonsense.

The costs of deliberate cultivation appear subtle, far-reaching, and poorly understood in any circumstances considered, from farming to parenting to anything in between. Being mindful or careful may not be enough to prevent associated costs, harm, from occurring."

Lives spent attempting to control an illusion evoke compassion. Lives spent attempting to share love evoke compassion. To one a bequest, the other to behold.

"Behold the universe as one and it is a vessel that can scarcely hold all love. Break it into pieces and the love runs between the cracks of likes and dislikes into a well of suffering."

"The four horsemen of the apocalypse of the human psyche:

fear, anger, pain, and banality."

"The sigh is the small death that opens space for the next inhaled life."

"You sit at the keyboard and wonder, “Who will get control of the fingers tonight?” “Is it the poet; the clown; the spirit; the child; the explanitararian; captain obvious?” Who does the muse, glancing at her batting order card, send to the plate with the game on the line? She smiles and says, “Sip your Chai tea awhile; I’m sure something will occur to us.” And you want very much to make love to her in that moment."

"The universe is providing all being in each moment, it is literally begging you to discover in each moment the totality of being, the ‘this is what I exist for’ each moment. A divine joke with a rolling punchline...did you get it? Did you get it? Did you get it? Over and over for all of form for all of totality."

"Once you notice, every inhaled breath is a bliss-saturated acknowledgement of being, a rhythmic dance with the universe, the moment of all connection, comfort, satisfaction, and yearning. And the exhale? An orgasm of giving from the soul. Lots of noticing to be done in this form. So little time."

"Collective Existentialism: The moment the totality of spirit is realized through the authenticity of all being. Who am us?"

"How much of the universe is analogous to an evening meadow filled with the brief, warm, pleasingly random glow of fireflies seeking their mates? Human lives? Creativity? Those seem auspicious starts."

"Have you ever wondered what lies beyond all conception? You do."

"Experiencing life in form serves nature, the manifest, the mother, through the relationship with the moment, creating and recreating

the world of now.

"Say formlessness with letters that emerge into forming words that emerge into forming thoughts that emerge into perception. None of that exists in formlessness.

Picture formlessness when neither color nor shape disintegrates for view. Hear formlessness when neither tone nor echo reaches consciousness. Touch formlessness; space touching space only more so. Love formlessness, this one can do here or there."

"I suspect that there is a point of observation of the totality of consciousness. This would be what we call God and would explain both the creator of all (that's what consciousness does, manifests form) and us in that image as mini-me points of consciousness observation."

"There is my awareness, a single point observing all thought, feeling, sensation and the universe, that is all. In this I have no Possessions or preferences, only a wondrous awareness that I can add love to the all, an all that fills my being like an imagined dream."

"Consciousness is not subject to the laws of physics."

"Consciousness emerged in this universe and all sentient expression is coming from that source point. When someone speaks or moves with intent, the source point is the origin of all being. This awareness tends to be fleeting for me."

"I am an instrument of consciousness, not the owner/operator."

"May I be the flute through which the breath of consciousness blows pure sweet notes of love and bliss. May I be the hollow chamber, surrounded by this skin, that the beats of my heart evoke rhythm sounded through the gentle hands of the divine drummer's hands. May I be the awakened intended motion of consciousness in form. May I be the hollowed gourd that carries the divine nectar of pure consciousness to the thirsty."

"What exploded in the big bang was consciousness. It exploded in dimensionality. And some was attached to matter. That's you.

For today. You cannot enslave spirit, but you can let it sing and dance."

"Maybe being human is divine artwork, a dab of matter and a swirl of spirit thrown out into the universe to become a unique expression of itself. Being a work of art takes a lot of the performance expectations off and allows the beauty of subjectivity to chase the popularity contest away."

Today's Human Hubris Award:
To the person who coined the phrase:
"Universal Remote"
Nice try.

"New World Order?

I'll have mine over easy please...

with a side of grace and a little love poured over the top."

"The goal of power is to deflect and distract executive functioning so that it does not attend to the inequities and injustice, the cruelties and abuses, the carelessness and lack of sensitivity that modern human behavior has developed into"

"The gifts of being if freely shared will transform being for the collective organism. It is the hoarding and leveraging of these gifts, even the withholding of offering from shame that is the basis of the alzeimers and cancer analogies of human being"

"What the Dormouse said: An unfed mind will consume your existence. The consumer society saturation of zombie stories is no accident. It is depth psychology."

"Fallacy of thought: human thought hatches concepts that are beyond the minds ability to fully grasp them. The resulting imperfect glances and partial truths are then subjectively formulated into opinions, decisions, and actions that, because of their imperfect nature, will in all likelihood at the

best marginalize our potential to pettiness and at the worst extinguish the species. Tragic-comic or not, we remain poignantly beautiful."

"Loving the threat is soul calculus. Solve that problem set and you can proceed to the next."

We fit our relational space in the universe like a puzzle piece. Who put me here now that I can see how I fit?"

At its most pristine, objective may be more accurately conceived of as generally accepted subjectivity. Objective appears like infinite in that it is intangible, which does not apparently limit its potential to bully folks."

"The process of disintegration of being: discernment begets desire begets worship begets consumption begets demise. Reincarnation suggests a rinse and repeat element to this formula, as does the infinite number of discernable elements of the whole."

"The dimension that we understand as time is subject to the dimension we understand as love. Time, through love, can be compressed

Or dilated, not just in 'timeless moments' or in 'endless boredom', but in forever samadhi glances where you are ejected from this

Illusion of being into something much more vast and real."

"The extremities of being are fueled by emotion. While possibly appealing for their cut to the chase hey look at me

Energy, they serve to up the ante as to what qualifies as a life experience compared to irrelevance. Don't know if

Sliding big piles of life into the irrelevant space makes sense."

"Culture seems to default as the accidental and haphazard governor of individual being to the degree you choose to be subservient to it, be you punk or priest, healer or heathen."

"The wide variety of 'things' with non-discrete values, everything from love to the stock market to weather can give pause to the reliance on certainty as a value."

"The false assumption of full perception degrades knowledge precipitously. Whether it is faulty thinking or bludgeoned communicative

Tools, it seems that very little that we hold true, even the foundations of self and identity, our internal registry code of being, are anything

Related to true, except perhaps in the most narrow and limited ways."

"The nature of projection dictates that the only truth is subjective and that all we believe is pure delusion in the same heady breath. The spectral nature of consciousness, from God to lunatic runs in a circular motion with no fixed points of identity other than self identification."

"Consensual reality only tells you the relative popularity of your delusion. Realizing this, the fear to experience your own reality as a unique human experience may fade."

"A lesson on individuality: when you mix all the wonderful watercolors together by using the same brush and never really rinsing, what results? Consensual reality works that way. The efforts to unify individual experience reek of the fear of being alone in your universe. Since it seems immutable that we are indeed held separate by our own minds from all else we observe..."

"I guess the debaters between black/white dichotomy and gray variability have failed to notice the rainbows of nature and the swirling colors of the human mind with equal lack of aplomb. Bully for them."

"The real challenge to now is to not be afraid to express all the love it might contain if you so desired. The real challenge to life is realizing that this now is constantly reoccurring and inviting you to be human, really really human. Like you were born to be. And there is nothing that love cannot love."

"Alone, a huddled species of selves, we value and in perspective it seems the solace of a blanket far too short and light for a night of fatally cold temperatures. We shiver in our collective belief in the power of dance to make

a world of love. And the indifference remains. As if nature is unimpressed with our intentions and holds them merely as temporal delusions to a species far too cerebral for their own good."

"For love or the greater indifference, the horror if not embraced strengthens in shadow. Integration of soul requires that the blessed maggots strip free the judgments and attachments that the scared of the dark and even more scared of the alone, alone alone, self has suffocated itself in."

"It may be the projections and pretends of our beautiful minds, but if indeed our universe is projection than we are far darker than our luminous ones would paint us and I suspect the unremembered dreams of a lifetime are the dreams beyond redemption."

"You will suffer life's poison to the degree that you are dys-synchronized, dys-integrated from your identity. Odd to think that one could dys-integrate from an identity that one self projects and creates and sustains, but there you go. The

suffering of the poison is self evident: you are not who you are. After the purges, after the pain, it may be so, but first you've got some dues to pay."

"That life experienced could be a divergent moment of expanding possibility, rather than a convergent response predicated by experience is forgotten as the ego develops but that doesn't mean it isn't still there waiting for you."

"The question isn't whether I will become unhinged, dislodged from my moorings, the assumptions of being that I falsely

Believe are me. The question is whether the universe that surrounds me, going through its own unhinging process will

Synchronize with me in my process. Typically these things occur in fits and starts, and maybe catastrophically fast."

"A wise man said:

"How much do humans know compared to all there is to know?

Like zero percent right?"

Epic! Keep swinging away kids,

I'm sure you'll get to 1% any day now!"

"Instead of looking for, labeling, and treating pathology in a person's mental health, we might look for, label and treat the contextual precursors in the environment. Or would that be too much for civilization to stomach?"

"All form appears bound by projection and relation; from this singular form one alchemizes their life experience, pulling random parts

Into an imagined narrative being, infecting the field with their noticing; this process seems an unaccounted debt to self and the singular

Form to which we serve. Is that enough to be mindful?"

"I love all form. I love all formlessness. I love all. See what consciousness can do?"

"Be the you that the universe had in mind when you and this moment came into being. The universe didn't hold back in selectively creating you through billions of years of development; don't hold back either. You are so special, indescribably so."

"There is no way to alter consciousness to the point where it is fully realized other than to fully realize it. All the other stuff is the Longing of the desperate, worthy of compassion, but not emulation. Like Bob Dylan said, "You can't buy a thrill."

"Faced with infinite scale, let's not be anthropocentric. Scale wasn't designed with us in mind. Universes may be atoms, atoms universes, or both."

"We couldn't complete the universal jigsaw puzzle without your piece."

"Compassion, fully engaged, knows no scale of being and may be experienced universal to quantum with no limitations in space/time dimensionality and human consciousness can alchemize this state at will. Wonderful stuff.

Until science can explain this coherently, I will happily accept it as pure magic."

"The quiet ecstasy of the realization I am surrounded by the divine seems the gift of the awareness that my creativity

is only the notation of occurrence and that I am continually surrounded by this same process occurring in others."

"Genetics vs. Environment: Nature and nurture sat down for a card game. Nature dealt the cards. Nurture decided the game, called out the rules and led the three of clubs. I laid down the hand that I was dealt, walked away from the game being played, and went to live my life."

"Nature seems process oriented. And if all the parallel universes are some Shiva-esque manifestation of the dream space of consciousness, as they appear, then the human species can preliminarily conclude that the continued collective existence of our tribe is dependent upon our intuitive collective

management of consciousness in the context of nature's process."

"Your gifts ARE your compensation. Live the life that allows them to flourish in gratitude. Share them fully and freely. Nothing that brings another to higher consciousness should be for sale. No thing. Free market creativity and you might just be surprised."

"Adoration may be the key to human relationships. Adore all being. Adore everyone. The place in the heart that adore emerges from is a very special place that cannot be denied, nor fatigued. Find it and free yourself to adore humanity, adore being, adore self in world. Give it a nice warm hug, then set it free. Adore!"

"That a marketing team can create an image that is so much more desirable than that which you are currently experiencing speaks to the magic of human creativity. That we cannot find that desire in the virtual now speaks to its dearth." You are surrounded by the all, feel free to select the parts that make your groove come alive, then breath in the beat and fly into the flow; it is all right here right now."

"Since satisfaction is an internally determined subjective state of being, it is omnipresent and you may choose to live every moment of being satisfied. Why we permit 'no such things' (internally determined subjective states of being) to influence us one way or the other is puzzling in a world we ostensibly try to 'improve', since to an alchemists view, we're already there."

Into the divine mirror of each others' eyes and seeking validation of existence; there is no wrong way to play that game."

"Regarding hearts: broken doesn't mean destroyed, it means freed. A heart tied to the slavish service of one's desire touches no one. A heart so thorough broken it turns to dust covers all with the gentlest breeze of intent."

"Grace abhors its own company, as dark seeks to differentiate from light. Enlightened community, the yogic community, religious communities, intellectual communities are scared children clinging to each other in an effort to validate their tenuous grasp to

existence. If your game doesn't play on the street, take it home."

"The analogous quality of the universe is the pleading lover, the desperate child, the compliant victim to be touched, held, and released. Our suffering merely reflects our dearth of empathy for our partner in this dance: the pleading lover gone to town, the desperate child grown and distant, the compliant victim state's witness."

"A Proposal: that the conversion of reality to words is enough to question the validity of any and all scientific study. Words both distill and dilute reality in commonly disregarded fashion."

"The process of mastery entails a process of enslavement. They are mirror functions."

"The resonance of the concept of avatar in gaming stems from its resemblance to the experience of life: the observer self, the self behind the thoughts, behind the perceptions, behind the senses and the drives is as removed from actual life experience as the gamer

playing Mario. And sometimes the controls work even less here."

"All of the justifications of civilization go back to empowering the mind. Civilization itself is an exercise in thinking how to make the human condition somehow better. Yet with all that mind power, I cannot conceive, nor google, a way in which civilization supports or somehow enhances being, where the human condition resides."

"Entertainment frightens me. When we are not in its presence are we removed from being? Is entertainment omnipresent and I only needed to attune my senses as it screams my name? Is it a need, a want, a desire? Reward or punishment for sentience? If passion does not dance with attention are we somehow living a lower plane life? Or am I only supposed to believe this so I can enliven the party?"

"Prophylactic stance is a way to describe a life that is built to sustain through avoidance. If I don't touch it, it won't affect me. If you've had to construct an impervious barrier, aren't you already affected? And there might always be

one more danger than barrier, leading to a life of constant barrier building and vigilance. New barriers/checking for leaks/disinfecting. Is that any way to be?"

"Comes to mind a notion that the homeopathic stance uses judo in life's dance that a prophylactic stance cannot. Avoidance seems intuitively non-curative, perhaps toxic. Medusa was killed with her own reflection; those who hid turned to stone. "Try to run, try to hide, break on through to the other side" as Jim Morrison would say..."

"The only gift I can see for our supplications to the all is not the paused moment of okay that we may hold and call life as our subconscious fights with the demons of madness at the gates of our awareness, shaving off the dying children, raped women, marginalized workers, and exploited planet from our conscious minds. A shinier gift, in sparkly paper, from a universe that valued sentience would be the opening of the gates of hell and madness so that when we buy this ticket to Disneyland, we get not only the illusion, to keep us safe, but thrilled, but also the real experience of being, shadows and all."

"if being can be assumed to have a constant value of meaning, then the disregarded meaning, that of the marginalized, may hold the relevance to our collective existence."

"Who am I now that only the future is remembered and only the past is dreamt?"

"There is a type of alone that is not time with yourself, it is time without yourself. This is a land of despair and timeless degradation. I appreciate it exists for me only in dreams. An enlightened shadow is very dark indeed."

"Who explained to us what and why to remember? Was there some informal process I missed? My planet of being feels lopsiding and in danger of tipping from the varied emphasis. This is not the way to cartograph life; burning the bad and filming the good and forgetting the rest. My planet is an unkempt disaster of subjective mapping; I might get lost around any corner."

"cling to life."

"The essence of being appears relational. The seminal relationship, the registry code of relationship, seems between self and self's thought content. From the dynamics of that relationship the experience of life results."

The over-arching human relationship is with desire. Every action appears predicated by desire and the fruits of your true desires surround you in full evidence of that which you may not realize. Whether the service to desire, for even forsaking desire is a form of desire, may be conceived of as an existential form of slavery or whether there may be a path or process embedded that serves a greater good or reaches a plane of existence where one could be freed of the bit and harness, we are left to choose, mostly guess I suppose. It seems that this choice, how to frame this lifelong conscious relationship to desire that becomes the touchpoint for all forms of convincing, marketing, religion, the moral and legal codes, dreams, intuitions, family, experiential reality all would speak to us that they understand and can provide us appropriate channel for our relationship with desire. On this court, the game of life may be played, nothing more.

"In true 99% awakening, we must first occupy our own existence, sitting in our central private space until all of those parts of our being (the 1% of the true whole) that have co-opted existence and marginalized the authentic expression of our lives have given each of us back that which was never theirs to take, reclaiming and neutralizing the power that has brutalized the very essence of being, the soul, from the moment we stopped recognizing it as the foundation of self and the divining tool of a just and happy life."

"You are an awakened, self-realized, enlightened etcetera being, whether you are immediately aware of this or not so much so; it is a state of being that is not subject to the space/time continuum. (Insert 4-G Verizon moment here, now.)"

"There are two states of consciousness: the relational and the non-relational. An awareness of non-relational consciousness, whether by conceiving or by direct experience while in this relational state can be very helpful in firmly grasping the totality of the relational state, particularly important when relating to the

thoughts and feelings and sensations that are so intimately yours, but yet not you."

"The determination of value in your relationship with life is the moment by moment coincidence of functionality and meaning to the self perceived reality."

"If being is all relevance, then you are free to dismiss all else as distracting background clutter. Attention focused to this degree, in sufficient amounts, would result in potential states of consciousness that are, as yet, difficult to imagine. A sort of nuclear fission of consciousness."

"Be the poem, the song, the improv performance art that streams from your ever-changing identity and surround yourself with those who have likewise given themselves to the performance with whole heart and open intent; they'll appreciate your stuff as well."

"Analogous: Human beings to human neuron cells. Meaning: Together we constitute the collective mind of humanity and our

sympathetic and asympathetic responses to collective humanity mimic brain neural action. Also meaning: you have a global civilization in your mind and you would be its God or something".

See the Birdie

Earth as in Mind: Electric charges fly from synapse to synapse as the great flocks migrate along millennially established pathways. Along these pathways self and god, identity and other manifest and are made real. In nature, mountains fall, rivers dry, courses change. And the human touch: the dams that flood, the draining to build fields, the cities built on unconsidered imminent domain. Gradually and at times in a moment a single bird, an entire flock, perhaps the species itself: adapt or die or both: as with self and god, even in fair stewardship of mind where the flight paths of the migratory routes of being itself are laid moment by moment in the course of a unique existence.

Experiencing life in form serves the unmanifest by calling forth in polyharmonic/polycacophonic voice and rhythm that which will

Awaken and emerge from our fierce dancing with now. All serve. The least aware and most aware serve in kind."

"The redrawn demarcation of duality: you occupy the point of observer awareness at the very core of your being. The rest, from your thoughts,

feelings body, senses, earth , wind, and fire, planets, stars, and quasars can be conceived of as the other, the universe. But the demarcation line starts the instant one exceeds the single point of awareness, not at the end of the tips of the fingers."

"The universe is magically divine and begging you to construe it as such because you manifest with your glance, voice and touch."

"Reflect on the world of man. Understand that all we have built, all we have done represents our collective best thinking. Consider two things: the external world reflects the inner-world of our thoughts in direct correlation, as our actions emerge from our ideas. Second, that the default cure for best thinking is probably 'better thinking' (getting out of the box/new paradigm etc.) a concept so counter-

intuitive it can't find a large enough red flag to wave."

Habituated to the Inconceivable: the suffering in a world flush with resources, the alternate harm and inanity of power and politics, the casual disregard for lives not ours, technology, nature, ourselves, the power of our consciousness to create, destroy, damn and bless. The very nature that creates our empirical subjective reality proceeds to blind us to its wonders. Awaken children!

Electric charges fly from synapse to synapse as the great avian flocks migrate along millennially established pathways.

Like stars and suns, other sentient beings have gravity effects in your experience, the closer, the higher the gravity. Our teachers and co-experiencers, they deserve the realization of their preciousness in my eyes in every moment.

we are our own horseman of the apocalypse...go humans. buy and sell. power and wealth. bad parenting. the collective delusion of nation-states. the inability to conceive of the quantum values of individual

behavior. is it too late to hunt and gather? 'fraid so kiddos.

Life: Are you composing your own or interpreting another's work? Are you sight reading? Have you memorized your part? Are you improvising? I look upon the moon-stricken night sky and bathed in billion year old fusion light I recognize the universe as a crazy score on an impossible scale and try to imagine I have the range to play it.

"So so hungry for joy, starving people...do you want joy? Realize that every moment you are creating being and you can do whatever you want in this form. Is that not enough??? Then go ahead and make the magic you wish to see with it....sheesh."

"Moods: Conjured, Alchemized, or Manufactured?"

"The option nature of suffering and yes pain allows that it be sampled in small discrete portions as the part of the vast epicurean delight of human experience that we bring forth manifest. The richness and spiciness of these particular delights, suffering and pain, leads me to consider the value of a gluttonous stance towards them. Are we so mindless, so un-creative, that we must gorge on this, the first yummy treat at the endless banquet of life experienced in form?"

"Guilty or innocent, captive or free, burdened or blessed, one is subject only to the degree one chooses. Just or not, you cannot punish nor harm those who are unattached to your games."

"At its foundational level, creativity, moment by moment, can be conceived of as the vector force towards or away from realized consciousness. Never let its value be understated or underappreciated."

"Are emotions particles or waves? Do thoughts follow quantum or traditional physics? How does the dreaming mind do the calculus necessary to mimic flight? Love, le raison d'etre hasn't been discovered yet. We cannot rest assured in anything and must find shelter in the unknown or concede the slavery of an empty existence. Fill up your space with yourself."

"The potential cost of ownership of one's emotions is a lifetime of service to the ego as it alternately propagandizes the future and revises history to fit the perceived contexts. There may be other ways to determine who you are and what it might mean, let alone what to spend life creating."

"Regarding feelings and emotion: Perhaps, given the individuality of topography of being that we seemingly possess, life is the Sisyphean boulder we are forced to squander the energy of being on, for the hubristic belief that we are somehow worthy of being the gods of emotion."

"The human mind is a flawed operating system. It relies on incomplete data from flawed sense organs and has a horribly subjective and incomplete data analysis 'system'. As a poetic experiential tool for the subjective being of semi-sentient life, it is ideally suited. As a determiner of truth, it is awkward at best and horrific and abusive much more commonly."

"It is lovely to see all the elemental pieces of what we call God milling about in semi-amnesiac states, looking to remember.

"Human perceptual power has a limited capacity, kind of like RAM in a computer and so the more past that populates any moment, the less of you is left to be present to the moment itself. Then of course, being human and all, we can import all sorts of future probabilities into the moment and spend our time worrying"

"The mind and the immune system have analogous systems. The majority of health symptoms are your immune systems reactions to the environment. The majority of your suffering is your minds reactions to the environment."

"Attachment to form? Ever-changing and ever-wonderful universe. Holding onto pieces a lifetime of moments costs. Alive only now."

"Form: less concrete and steel structure, than momentary expression of universal being. When seen through these eyes, awe, wonder, and a wave of full compassion bathe and

nourish my heart. Life slips through my fingers, as it was meant to."

"How tall I am lends itself to quantitative measurement, at least when I am upright, although the ramifications are both infinite and most meaningless. How I experience my being can only be measured qualitatively and through a very subjective lens, anything else is abusive."

"Abuse and hypocrisy are the primary beneficiaries of ideologies. Ideologies are smoke and mirror constructs manipulated at will and in evolutionary processes to serve the desires of their rulers, those with power within that framework: so you get Killer Christians, Oligarchic Democrats, Plutocratic Republicans, and Elitist Yoga people without batting an eye. Ideological thinking or system design needs to be viewed with extreme skepticism at all times, more so when you are a believer."

Only the most awkward hacks and viruses are evident to the computer. Many are not even evident to the computer operator. The mind is

a very very complex computer that is not immune to hacks and viruses, particularly from those in power. If you trust your mind to navigate this experience, wouldn't it be important to check for malware?"

"Bless the activists on both sides fueled by their subjective righteousness and justice they pull the knot of human being as tightly as they can. Those who might untie the knot drift away with their forks and tweezers and dextrous fingers. The universe rummages in the drawer for the sharp scissors."

"Select the more fair version:
1. Sheepdogs are classified by breed. Their characteristics are understood to be the result of selective breeding and the best use of these characteristics are expressed through environment, including training to strengths.
2. Persons with ADHD are classified by disease. Understood to be brain dysfunction. Forced into non-adaptive environments and given medication."

For any given homogenaety of human species (cultural, etc) the degree of individuals afflicted with mental health problems will accurately reflect the degree of types of

pathology inherent in said homogenaety. Universe within universe without."

"Coping implies a deficit in human being for all of us that I am not willing to concede."

"The mind, conscious of its own demise and convinced that control will forestall the inevitable seeks to delude the true self into drinking the kool-aid and joining the Jim Jones collectively deluded society where we can burn carbon and oppress our brothers and sisters. Is this the life you signed up for, or is there more?"

"Who you are may indeed be the only thing you ever determine beyond a guess or an estimate in your entire life. Not that you're given any clues or anything...more like distractions, distortions, delusions, illusions and the like, but the alchemy of self appears to be the grail of being."

"While it is miraculous that all of us possess the spark of a heroic ideal as part of our human make-up, it is tragic that it would be necessary,

an imperative, to need it to rise above a suffocating and toxic world. What could resiliency be used for if it wasn't needed just to stay afloat?"

"They make fun of 'hoarders', who are only emulating corporations (who hoard money and power) who are only emulating cancer cells (who value growth to the exclusion of life). That parallel process can generate such mixed reviews only a critic can love."

"You need no license to amuse with parlor tricks, nor do the true magicians bother with such detail; only performers for money need the validation and protection of a licensing guild, their work neither amusing nor magic."

The accountant uses numbers for numbers; the mathematician uses numbers for tools; the computer programmer uses numbers for virtual creation; the physicist uses numbers to decipher nature; perhaps a calculation for love may unfold with a pile of bloody pencil stubs and a mountain of crumpled scratch paper sitting at the feet of the supercomputer that sucked all of the universe's life and energy to make the determination. There seems a

degree of superfluicity to figuring out sometimes.

"The Big Bang, as conceptualized, showed us that the entire universe can fit within the smallest imaginable piece of consciousness. That the entirely of being fits together in virtual nothingness may comfort those who feel lonely when not squished together and merged with the whole universe, right?"

"Dream large, at the height of your imagined longings seems but a trifle for universal will. The longings of spirit will be kindly indulged as such."

"If you are waiting for the illusional scales of time to drop off before your eyes, please stop. Waiting requires time."

"Do you still suppose you are mortal? Be kind today for only your supposition is mortal; the illusion will fade."

"I've got a new job! I now get to open gifts all day long. Gifts specially for me. I'm surrounded by them, so many I can't possibly ever finish, but the job is so beautiful I don't mind. All I have to do is notice. And the universe is hiring! And if you're reading this then you are one of my gifts."

"Dance is the physical articulation of sound. Sound is motion heard, not seen."

"May you be gifted with the wisdom of the birds; moved to song by the return of the sun."

"In my dreams when I was young I needed wings to fly. Now by will alone."

"Love can be alchemized through an unfolding universe. It doesn't need a sentient entity with opposing thumbs texting its blueprint."

"Kindness is love attuned by empathy and tempered by altruism; a more elegant expression of humanity escapes me."

"To awaken the world we have to awaken our authentic being in critical mass proportions to ourselves, internally.

"Unable to clearly recall, I suspect that my entire existence was signed and sealed for the moment I looked into your eyes and recognized my soul."

"For a moment to last forever you must move away from it at the speed of light, forever."

With the divergence and insistence of the various right thought movements, highlighted by either political party, the various religions, and science, particularly the cognitive-behavioral branch of psychology which has so helpfully designated our thoughts as functional or dysfunctional or distorted or delusional, it can be clear that no method or style of thought management can be viewed as more than a desperate attempt by its proponents to gain enough consensus to somehow validate their lifetime spent doing whatever they do. What I find distressing is the pressure, judgment, and marginalization they place on all those who represent another way to be human. There are no optimal or preferred states of being. Only human-ness being human-ness. Leave each other alone, let each other be yourselves and appreciate how spirit can be brought forth in so many wonderful forms.

"The point of being known as the observer ('you' when it's all compressed into our operating systems mp3 translation) may perhaps serve the universe not as the chronicler of all that is 'real', but instead as a fulcrum between the concrete and the quantum, the conscious and the unconscious, Shiva and Shakti, the 'real' and the 'imagined' (manifest and potential?)."

"Consensual-nonconsensual reality is the sliding scale of payment made for the ongoing relationship to our thoughts."

"If facebook and google give us unique perspectives based on our habits, is there any doubt that our mind and the universe have a

more subtle and sophisticated app that does the same thing?"

Disengeniousness seems to be a powerful survival attribute in a world where nothing is really true to begin with."

"That nonsense can give sense a good run for the money and sometimes even nose out a victory in the shadow of the wire if the jockey's willing to go to the whip in midstretch and ride through the line is reassuring to the intuition that roots for nonsense even when it isn't in the race at all."

"The coercive and desperate flavor of consensual reality concerns me. Why are we constantly forcing people to our point of view? Scared to be a species of one?"

"questions lie trapped, like pawns or prole, between the inquisitor and the answer, their executioner whom when they meet they will exist no more. don't seek to figure yourself out too blithely; it comes with a final reckoning. an enigma, even if impertinent, may be immortal.

is the elixir of eternal youth to be unanswerable?"

Why we needed the verb 'to be' and all it's forms: so we could create the universe, over and over again.

Mother, a face that I once thought was mine. Eyes of the universe. Mouth of all words. Universe birthing universe, the mirror goes smoky with self awareness. Has the universe forgotten its mother? Or does it call out in the night, aloneness awakening memory?

Beauty's Constant: Beauty is relational to life. Sensorially, contextually, allegorically for a thing to be labeled beautiful it has to resonate with an aspect of the perceiver's life.

Life permutates like music in its possibilities, each song in context to all others in time and space. Which is the analogy? And what's that tune you're playing sister?

Who we are: we are who we are it seems, mostly in the moments between when we're aware of who we are, when we are being without filtering.

When you emerge from the oneness, from the darkness into flesh, fear not. All is universe still. Mark well the callings of this flesh, for food, comfort, warmth, and later flesh, for if unheeded, these calls will haunt all being. Nature will exact her cost for the gift of being. You are not in a cage of self, but in a dance with all life.

They used to be existentialists; then they died. The realizing is done here and now.

Love? Letting people be who they are and recognizing them as miraculous. Big love? The universe. Starts? In you. You won the impossible lottery of existence. Won something more rare than imagination can fathom. It's yours, your only need is to exist.

"When the nuclear physicists tell us we have nothing to worry about, the nice thing is that on a metaphysical level, they're correct."

Staring hard into the fog of being, the mind emerges familiar shapes from the gloom.

Hit and keep moving: The opposite of being is knowing.

Close attention to the thoughts that rise unvarnished from the place between sleep and waking; there seems to be a special truth to them.

When you came into being, every gift you would ever need was yours. The universe was yours alone to experience in this form. Have you forgotten? Did the grown-ups bury that truth? What are you really hungry/lonely/angry/fearful/longing for? Only remembering. Only remembering.

Simply being: so cool there doesn't have to be a point to it. Pass it on.

"Nothing travels in a linear fashion because we're whirling swirling in a dancing universe. Straight is an illusion; its belief a delusion."

"Emotion: the resonant love that awareness brings, an odd subjective proof of a level of universal function beyond our current ability to configure. Feelings: the inexpertly and somewhat selfishly manipulated emotional energy by ego through desire."

"The more of self one can dissolve, the more of universe one can access. Still enough and you can hear a baby cry across the world, a song to god in a voice that needs no translation, the gratitude and relief of the plants as they are touched by the morning sun. A star's first breath of hydrogen fire. Still enough. Still enough to be."

"May our collective soul open to the stillness your songs make space for in Palm Springs

tonight. I love your humble soul, like a child who stumbled across the shiny stone of divine love and tucked it in his pocket along with all the other treasures of a life's wandering."

"Humans are the subjective aspect of God's omniscience. Never doubt your own divinity or the criticality of your being."

"Perhaps the best analogy for the singularity of the All is the totality of being that surrounds us, unfiltered and adored."

"that we aspire so may be shining beauty; that we merely be truly resplendent."

"The universe of this moment is all inclusive of the universe of that moment. Why do you feel differently now?"

"The breeze of a hummingbird's wings is the Dom Perignon of air."

"In the place where there is just me, there is no me."

"Finders keepers? When I determined that my purpose was to find wonder in being all being became wonderful."

"Consciousness seems only recognizable through its neuro-chemical movement. If it stood still it would blend into the background. Like music with no notes."

"Conscious life: awareness in the flow state of the integrated context of universal unfolding. And that's it."

"There was once a society that bribed its empaths with gifts of prestige and riches to express compassion at its self-imposed subjective suffering so that its members were absolved, not of the heroic, but of the merely humane acts of self-efficacy. That society (and its empaths) soon perished."

"If an existential context can be determined then the occurrence of the event is non-pathological by definition. That cures quite a few ills."

Compassion may be conceived of as the awareness that all humans, all conscious life, whether it is karmic or nature/nurture or Truman Show paranoid nightmare is moment by moment acting out an elaborate and complex caricature of who they think they are supposed to be. Inspiration for their role is drawn from a variety of demographic, cultural, biological, and conscious and unconscious prompting and from this infinite ongoing calculus, we act what we believe is our identity. Compassion is realizing this is not who we are; that the supposed identity is false, and loving each as their own expression of who they

believe themselves to be, knowing that their true identity is the single-pointed vastness of the all.

"Parallel universe as a concept may find its nesting place in the similar, but unique perspectives of all conscious life with various relational matrices, proximity, like species, and other cultural determinants contributing to the differentials. Some very very similar, some very diverse, all unique, each a universe of being unto itself."

Being is the gift.
(Do the math: what % of the universe experiences life?)

Sentience is the potential to realize the gift.
(Do the math: what % of the living universe realizes it is alive?)

Simply existing is such a boon that in itself it justifies bliss. Existence is a miracle of possibility that is beyond all odds and you experience it.

Even better: no one else gets to experience life

from your perspective: you got the only ticket to this show. The universe belongs to you and you alone. All being is yours from your perspective. Your child smiles for you. The stars shine for you. The sun warms you.

Habituation Considerations: How much of this realization do you need to be grounded in it consistently? Is knowing it once enough? Refreshing every five minutes? Do you need specific practices to support the realization as foundational to being? Can this point of realization withstand tv news and junk food and cacophonic lifestyle and ethyl alcohol in your experience, or do these or other elements distract or diffuse the neuro-chemical signature that absolute belief in those two thoughts generates?

Societal Influences:
1. A fallacy that this miracle of being is in some way contingent to a certain behavioral/though subset.
2. A fallacy that there is some preferential function/state.

Existence is wonderful. It is full of wonder. You are witness to the wonder, the complete wonder of being, all of it.

Changing the World 2012

1. Filling and being always filled with this realization will (I hypothesize) result in a neuro-chemical signature of extreme wellbeing. Determine your individual dose level...what kind of a life do you need to sustain this simple realization?

2. Living in this state of preternatural joy (important side note, under the guidance of this realization, sadness is not banished, nor despair, these are worshipped under the same bliss/love/joy that everything else is) will naturally result in a diminishment of consumer culture, aggressor culture, etc. as hunger to be beyond the gift of simply being will dissipate gently.

3. Sharing the groove deliberately: your kindness and compassion for the experience and all the beings that fill it will generate buzz. MP3 people, iGen people know how to spread buzz. Saying out loud this is your operating system will spread the buzz. The more the merrier.

4. Neurological voodoo: brains grasping to figure out who, what, where, when, why and how...hungry brains trying to stay safe and sane will meet grounded happy joyful brains full of self-realized peace and calm. Feeling no threat from the grounded brains, the hungry brains will shift in response to begin to entrain with

the brains that realize and appreciate that every second of existence is a miracle beyond imagining and a gift beyond reconciling.
5. The 'I scream you scream we all scream for ice cream' moment of tipping point where the collective human consciousness shifts into a lovingkindness emergence into a temporally realized divinity.

Ultimate free will: unblinded by chronology, the souls incarnation is a full commitment to the folly, pain, and beauty of imagining heaven on this physical plane; that the soul commits: I will be a child to these parents; I will go to this school; I will suffer these fates. That the soul still goes forth, into the mix, makes all humans, all sentient life indescribably beautiful to me, realizing that choice is made.

We loved the sun so much for it's warmth and safety and missed it so much at night, we took little brother fire home to bed with us. That was the night we split from nature and began to tune out the fundamental messages of the universe, starting with the songs of the stars.

Beautiful paradox: I am absolutely committed to authenticity of self. I have verly little idea of who that might be.

the totality of all dimension belongs to one who walks no path

all language is metonymy for the divine.

The Jimmy Hoffa grounding technique: set both feet in concrete. Life will go swimmingly.

the moment is all-encompassing and I am infinite within it.

Is the depth of a moment so easily plumbed that we have time to play pretend with memories, hopes, and fears? When I am gifted immersion I have yet to touch bottom.

Consensus has no correlation to truth, nor right, nor best. Scared fragile egos glomming on to groupthink...lemmings.

Adorative compassion, the compassion of adoration. This. Is. It.

Transmuting the illusional poisons of external phenomena to love we are the gods of our faiths. Any other fate and we are the ghosts and demons of our nightmares, haunting present and future trying to reconnect with the real of our being.

Melancholia savored adds depth and hue to the life experience.

Children of trauma validate their mothers suffering. They say to their mothers and the world with their behavior that the pain was real and undeserved.

Human tendency to build fallacious constructs between fallacies is either endearingly creative or #epicfail stupid. Our minds are so completely incapable of their most basic operating assumptions ("I see all that is before me.") that we appear to have no choice in the

matter. Still. No wonder Einstein's hair stuck out so much.

Integrity, when drawn from shallow waters, must be cleansed of the impurities of ego and power or its use will be tainted. Deep-source integrity selflessly serves the permanent unchanging face of being.

my mind is a speck in the vastness of my being. it cannot in any comprehensive sense surround who I am. to use it as such can confound and confuse.

Words do not describe what's real, they describe your perceptions and thoughts. What is real remains hidden behind the veil of the mind.

I meditated in a dream last night. I understand the mathematical concept of exponential differential a bit better this morning.

The only place the universe is ever any different is in your head.

Your distress has a sponsor. It's....you! Mine does too, it's me!

Atheists are God's favorite children because they get it. Even those who attempt to worship everything are guilty of only worshipping that which they might notice. Those who worship nothing above anything else have factored in their relative imperfection in a God pleasing way.

You are a super hero. Your super power is a compassion beam. Whatever you focus it on will fill you with love. Start with yourself first. You've spent so much time and effort filling your life with bullshit instead of moments. You were not told. You didn't know any better. You can reclaim your magic. It is okay now. Shine that beam inside.

I have no idea what I mean and only the slightest sense of what I've said until it settles into someone making meaning and finds its way back to me.

the fact that my consciousness continues to project a physical presence is evidence I have not yet remembered my identity. whoever would ever miss me never knew me either.

I always thought of Jungian shadow as something lurking in the recessed corners of my mind, however since this universe is a projection of my being, I am able to conceive of shadow as that which is occurring in my universe to which I avert my attention. Hence the starving people, sexual abuse, war, greed, environmental abuse, wasted being and all the assorted usual suspects of an amok civilization that perhaps trouble us, but only to the extent that we resent the energy necessary to turn the other way: shadow.

Therapy gossip: From my relational feminist standpoint, I get a chuckle out of existentialism and CBT pretending to be strangers when they're clearly in bed with other. Where does existentialism spring from if not the beliefs and thoughts of cognition? Where does CBT focus, if not in the heart of the existential problem? Stop pretending, we know you're having an affair...

It isn’t the world that crushes the human spirit, the magic of being, only your belief that this is so, a much more intractable problem.

Your life is all about what you type in your search engine

Corporations as people will act in their self interest without the maturing values of mortality to temper their accumulation drive.

If we can manifest love, what else is there worth doing?

Kindness is love attuned by empathy and tempered by altruism; a more elegant expression of humanity escapes me.

Postface:

Want more?

Go to: Lulupublishing.com

Search: Scott Dudley

Or: dudley64@msn.com

Although I'm not the quickest on the uptake on email…

Or: https://www.facebook.com/dyttocs

Or: twitter or linkedin or…

www.ingramcontent.com/pod-product-compliance
Ingram Content Group UK Ltd.
Pitfield, Milton Keynes, MK11 3LW, UK
UKHW041920190726
13854UKWH00003B/1342

9 781304 615862